Craters of

**A Guide to Craters of the Moon
National Monument and Preserve
Idaho**

Produced by Craters of the Moon Staff

**U.S. Department of the Interior
Washington, D.C.**

"A place of color and silence. . . ." Robert Limbert, 1924

Cover Photo: "Volcanic Palette"—David R. Clark © 2010

Craters of the Moon
A Guide to Craters of the Moon
National Monument and Preserve, Idaho

Produced by the Staff of Craters of the Moon
National Monument and Preserve

Library of Congress Control Number:
2010903465
ISBN 978-0-615-36038-6

Part 1

Exploration and Preservation

Craters of the Moon was so named because at one time people thought this landscape resembled the moon's surface.

Light playing on cobalt blue lavas of the Blue Dragon Flows caught the inner eye of explorer Robert Limbert: "It is the play of light at sunset across this lava that charms the spectator. It becomes a twisted, wavy sea. In the moonlight its glazed surface has a silvery sheen. With changing conditions of light and air, it varies also, even while one stands and watches. It is a place of color and silence. . . ."

Limbert explored the Craters of the Moon lava field in Idaho in the 1920s and wrote those words for a 1924 issue of National Geographic Magazine. "For several years I had listened to stories told by fur trappers of the strange things they had seen while ranging in this region," wrote Limbert, a sometime taxidermist, tanner, and furrier from Boise, Idaho. "Some of these accounts seemed beyond belief." To Limbert, it seemed extraordinary "That a region of such size and scenic peculiarity, in the heart of the great Northwest, could have remained practically unknown and unexplored. . . ." In 1920, on his third and most ambitious trek, Limbert and W. L. Cole were at times left speechless by the lava landscape they explored. Limbert recounted his impressions in magazines and newspaper articles whose publication was influential in the area being protected under federal ownership. In 1924, part of the lava field was proclaimed as Craters of the Moon National Monument, protected under the Antiquities Act by the National Park Service (NPS). It was created to preserve "a weird and scenic landscape peculiar to itself." The boundary has been adjusted and the monument enlarged since then. In 1970, a large part of the national monument was designated by Congress as the Craters of the Moon Wilderness.

The most recent expansion occurred in 2000 when, by Presidential Proclamation, the monument was enlarged by the addition of Bureau of Land Management (BLM) lands that were designated as a new national monument and preserve. The new boundaries now encompass an area about the size of Rhode Island. The size of the monument was increased in order to ensure that the Great Rift—a 52-mile-long volcanic fissure—and the massive flows that issued from it were protected as one landscape.

Today, the National Park Service along with the Bureau of Land Management cooperatively manage this greatly expanded monument. These two agencies within the Department of the Interior work together to enhance public service and protect nationally significant natural and cultural resources, while retaining many of the traditional uses of the land.

Until 1986, little was known about Limbert except for those facts recounted above. That year, however, a researcher compiling a history of the national monument located Limbert's daughter in Boise. The daughter still possessed hundreds of items, including early glass plate negatives, photographs, and manuscripts by her father that shed more light on his life, the early days of Idaho, and Craters of the Moon. Some of these photographs served as blueprints for the NPS in the rehabilitation of fragile spatter cone formations that had deteriorated over the years of heavy human traffic. The Limbert collection has been fully cataloged by Boise State University curators and has already proven to be a valuable resource to historians interested in Limbert and this fascinating part of Idaho. Preservation of the area owes much to Limbert's imaginative advocacy in the true spirit of the West in its earlier days.

Local legends, beginning in the late 1800s, held that this area resembled the surface of the moon, on which—it must now be remembered—no one had then walked! Geologist Harold T. Stearns first used the name Craters of the Moon when he suggested to the NPS, in 1923, that a national monument be established here. Stearns found "the dark craters and the cold lava, nearly destitute of vegetation" similar to "the surface of the moon as seen through a telescope." The name Craters of the Moon would stick after Limbert adopted it in National Geographic Magazine in 1924. Later that year the name became official when the area was set aside by President Calvin Coolidge as a national monument.

Like some other areas in the National Park System, Craters of the Moon has lived to see the name that its early explorers affixed to it proved somewhat erroneous by subsequent events or findings. When Stearns and Limbert called this lava field Craters of the Moon, probably few persons actually thought that humans might one day walk on the moon and see its surface firsthand. People have now walked on the moon, however, and we know that its surface does not, in fact, closely resemble this part of Idaho. Although the moon's surface is composed of the same type of rock and it retains some original volcanic features, most of its craters were formed by the impact of meteorites.

Moonscape or not, early fur trappers avoided the lava flows by taking a route already established by Native Americans along the base of the Pioneer Mountains. This trail was destined to become part of Goodale's Cutoff, an alternative route on the Oregon Trail that pioneers in wagon trains used in the 1850s and 1860s. Many adjectives used to describe this scene—weird, barren, exciting, awe-inspiring, monotonous, astonishing, curious, bleak, and mysterious—still apply. It is not difficult today to see why pioneering folk intent on wresting a living from the land passed quickly through this volcanic terrain.

This strange landscape first known as a "curiosity" became better understood as a series of dedicated geologists came to study the monument's lava formations. Several generations of geologists, beginning with Israel C. Russell in 1901 and Harold T. Stearns in the 1920s, developed a deeper understanding of the area's volcanic ori-

Next two pages: The showy blazingstar grows on the slopes of cinder cones and blooms in late summer. These flowers close their petals during the heat of the day so that the amount of water transpired is reduced.

gins. As geologists unravel the geologic story, the apparent otherworldliness of Craters of the Moon has retreated—but not entirely. The National Aeronautics and Space Administration (NASA) brought the second set of astronauts who would walk on the moon to this alien corner of the galaxy before their moonshot. Here they studied the volcanic rock before embarking on their own unearthly adventure.

Most types of volcanic features in the park can be seen quite readily by first stopping at the visitor center and then driving the Loop Road. Far more features can be seen by walking the interpretive trails found along this route. Still more await those who invest the time required to come to feel the mysterious timelessness and raw natural force implicit in this expansive lava field. Many travelers are en route to Yellowstone National Park and spend only a couple of hours visiting Craters of the Moon. This is ironic because the hot spot now under the Earth's crust at Yellowstone National Park is the same one that created Craters of the Moon. In fact, Craters of the Moon represents what Yellowstone's landscape may resemble in the future, and both areas provide insight into what happens when the Earth's unimaginable inner forces erupt to its surface.

Although Idaho is famous for forests, rivers, and scenic mountain wilderness, its Snake River Plain region boasts little of these attributes. This plain arcs across southern Idaho from the Oregon border to the Yellowstone area at the Montana-Wyoming border. It marks the trail of the passage of the Earth's crust over an unusual geologic heat source that now brings the Earth's incendiary inner workings so close to its surface near Yellowstone. This heat source fuels Yellowstone's bubbling, spewing, spouting geothermal wonders. Craters of the Moon stands as a geologic prelude to Yellowstone and a window into the Earth's fiery secrets.

When did all this volcanism at Craters of the Moon happen? Will it happen again? According to Mel Kuntz and other U.S. Geological Survey geologists who have conducted extensive field research at Craters of the Moon, the volcanic activity forming the Craters of the Moon lava field probably started only 15,000 years ago. The last eruption in the volcanic cycle ended about 2,000 years ago, about the time that Julius Ceasar ruled the Roman Empire.

Craters of the Moon is a dormant, but not extinct, volcanic area. Its sleeping volcanoes could become active again in the near future. One of the largest earthquakes of the last quarter century in the contiguous United States shook Idaho's tallest mountain, Borah Peak, just north of the monument in 1983. When it did, some geologists wondered if it might initiate volcanic activity at Craters of the Moon. It did not. According to Kuntz, however, this is no reason not to expect another volcanic eruption here soon—probably "within the next 1,000 years."

Today's Craters of the Moon National Monument and Preserve encompasses the Craters of the Moon lava field as well as the smaller Wapi and Kings Bowl lava fields. Extending southeastward from the Pioneer Mountains, the monument boundary encloses a series of deep fissures, volcanic cones, and numerous lava flows that collectively make up the Great Rift Volcanic Rift Zone. The Great Rift itself is a series of parallel cracks in the Earth's crust that can be traced for more than 50 miles across the Snake River Plain. Recent volcanism marks much of its length. You can explore the Great Rift and some of its volcanic features via the monument's seven-mile-Loop Road. Along the Loop Road, you will find spatter cones, cinder cones, lava flows, lava caves, and an unexpected variety of wildflowers, shrubs, trees, and wildlife. Beyond the Loop Road is a vast and little traveled region of stark volcanic features flanking the Great Rift. The Craters of the Moon Wilderness and Preserve offer a challenge to serious hikers and explorers—latter day Robert Limberts—who are prepared for rugged wilderness travel.

Despite its seeming barrenness, Craters of the Moon is indeed home to a surprising diversity of

Pages 14-15: The monument was named in 1924, long before humans walked on the moon. Although we now know more about the moon's actual surface, the monument's name still rings true. Certainly, the barren, jagged lava terrain provides a feeling of looking at an unearthly landscape.

Astronauts Eugene Cernan, Joe Engle, Alan Shepard, and Edgar Mitchell, visited the monument to study the geology and get a feeling for traveling over the rough, expansive lava before going to the moon.

Astronaut on the Moon

Astronauts
Eugene Cernan and
Joe Engle

plant and animal life. As Limbert noted in 1924: "In the West, the term 'Lava Beds of Idaho' has always signified a region to be shunned by even the most venturesome traveler—a land supposedly barren of vegetation, destitute of water, devoid of animal life, and lacking in scenic interest. In reality, the region has slight resemblance to its imagined aspect. Its vegetation is mostly hidden in pockets, but when found consists of pines, cedars, junipers, and sage-brush: its water is hidden deep in tanks or holes at the bottom of large 'blow-outs' and is found only by following old Indian or mountain sheep trails or by watching the flight of birds as they drop into these places to quench their thirst. The animal life consists principally of migrant birds, rock rabbits, woodchucks, black and grizzly bears: its scenery is impressive in its grandeur."

Years of patient record-keeping by scientists have fit numbers to Limbert's perceptive observations. The number of species identified includes more than 800 plants, 2,000 insects, 10 reptiles, over 200 birds, 59 mammals, and four amphibians. With few exceptions, the monument's denizens live mostly under conditions of great environmental stress.

Near constant winds, breeze-to-gale in strength, sweep across the lava rock to rob moisture from all living things. Scant soils, low levels of precipitation, the inability of cinder cones to hold rainwater near the surface, and the heat of the summer sun—intensified by heat-absorbing black lavas—only aggravate such moisture theft. Cinder surfaces register summer soil temperatures of over 150°F and show a lack of plant cover. Much of the land within the monument is sparsely vegetated.

When combined with the barren and torturous lava, these extremely harsh environmental conditions make Craters of the Moon one of the most inhospitable places on earth. This may sound bleak and unappealing, but it is these same characteristics that make the area unique and the visitor experience quite memorable. To both preserve and conserve this unusual landscape is difficult because any management mistakes tend to be long-lasting.

The responsibility for reducing or eliminating a variety of different impacts falls on a diverse group of scientists and agency personnel. These experts share common goals to keep all features as natural as possible (preservation) or to create a sustainable habitat where a variety of uses can take place with minimal damage to the ecosystem (multiple use). Some of the concerns that must be dealt with at Craters of the Moon include:

Exotic Plants. Invasive, exotic plants such as knapweed, cheatgrass, and leafy spurge have established themselves within the monument. These invaders are crowding out native plants and have profound effects upon the function of natural systems. To control or eliminate these plants, the NPS and BLM use a variety of methods including herbicides, biological control agents, and the physical removal of non-native plants.

Wildfire. Extensive wildfires have burned large tracts of sagebrush-steppe habitat and created exotic grasslands by altering entire plant communities. However, fire also plays an important role in the maintenance of some vegetative types and helps maintain habitat diversity. NPS and BLM staff work together to prevent wildfires and to plan how the agencies should react before, during, and after wildfire events.

Hunting. Hunting is permitted in the BLM-administered Monument and the NPS Preserve but prohibited in the original NPS Monument. In both cases, managers are trying to provide a positive user experience—hunting or wildlife viewing—while maintaining healthy populations of wildlife.

Protection of Geologic Resources. The lava looks indestructible, but it is actually very delicate. Walking on the lava flows causes the brittle surface to break, climbing the spatter cones destroys their walls, and walking or driving off-trail or off-road can cause irreparable damage. These problems are addressed through the use of signage, barriers, site restoration and educational materials. In cases where the destruction is severe or predictable, access may be restricted to prevent further resource damage.

Caves. All caves, because of their very fragile nature, are designated by law to be managed under strict standards. Cave features such as stalactites and stalagmites (lava or ice) are easy targets for vandals and cave wildlife such as some bats and cave beetles are considered sensitive species. In the Loop Road area of the monument, the use of the caves by visitors has been promoted by making some of them easily accessible. In other cases, use has been restricted or prohibited to protect critical cave resources.

Species of Special Concern. Species with "special status" include all plants and animals that occur within the monument that are sensitive, threatened, or endangered. In an attempt to maintain an ecosystem that mirrors the plant and animal communities prior to major alterations by humans, monument managers are most concerned about any species that has the potential to disappear. Unfortunately, some species like the grizzly and bighorn sheep that once populated the monument are already gone.

In managing for these species, the main goal is to prevent the destruction of critical habitat associated with their well-being. Plants that receive special attention include the obscure phacelia (one of Idaho's rarest plants) and Picabo milkvetch. Wildlife of concern include animals such as the greater sage-grouse, pika, gray wolf, Townsend's big-eared bat, kit fox, bald eagle, western toad, blind cave leiodid beetle, Brewer's sparrow, sage thrasher, and pygmy rabbit.

Other Resource Concerns. The list of other crucial concerns at Craters of the Moon involve less obvious resources; air quality, soil, soundscapes (elimination of unnatural noise), and preservation of cultural resources (pre-historic and historic sites). Even unnatural light at night is an intrusion on the natural scene that managers seek to protect. Monitoring programs have been developed to track changes in the condition of key resources serving as "vital signs" of ecosystem health and to determine if managers are fulfilling the monument's mandate.

The difficulty involved in protecting the monument's resources would certainly appeal to Limbert who reveled in challenges. History has justified the importance Limbert attached to the preservation of this landscape. Publicity arising from his explorations led to creation of the National Monument. Furthermore, that publicity put forth a rather heady claim that history has unequivocally borne out: "Although almost totally unknown at present," Limbert prophesied in 1924, "this section is destined some day to attract tourists from all across America. . . ."

Every year hundreds of thousands of visitors fulfill Robert Limbert's prophecy.

Part 2

From Moonscape to Landscape

Rift Volcanism on the Snake River Plain

A 400-mile-long arc known as the Snake River Plain cuts a swath from 30-to 125-miles-wide across southern Idaho. Idaho's official state highway map, which depicts mountains with shades of green, shows this arc as white because there is comparatively little variation here compared to most of the state. Upon this plain, immense amounts of lava from within the Earth have been deposited by volcanic activity dating back more than 14 million years. However, some of these lavas, notably those at Craters of the Moon National Monument and Preserve, emerged from the Earth as recently as 2,000 years ago. Craters of the Moon contains some of the best examples of basaltic volcanism in the world. To understand what happened here, you must understand the Snake River Plain.

Basaltic and Rhyolitic Lavas. Magma, the molten rock material beneath the surface of the Earth, is called lava when it reaches the surface. The lavas which erupted on the Eastern Snake River Plain were mainly of two types classified as basalt and rhyolite.

Basaltic and rhyolitic lavas formed in two different stages of volcanic activity. Younger basaltic lavas mostly lie atop older rhyolitic lavas. Drilling to depths of almost two miles near the plain's midline, geologists found one-half mile of basaltic lava flows lying atop more than 1½ miles of rhyolitic lava. How much deeper the rhyolitic lavas may extend is not yet known.

This combination—a thinner layer of younger basaltic lavas lying atop an older and thicker layer of rhyolitic lava—is typical of volcanic activity associated with an unusual heat phenomenon inside the Earth that some geologists have described as a mantle plume. The mantle plume theory was developed in the early 1970s as an explanation for the creation

What last happened here about 2,000 years ago looked much like this photograph of a volcanic eruption in Hawaii. Bubbling, pooling, and flowing lava blanketed the land as molten materials gushed out on the Earth. Most of the volcanic phenomena preserved at Craters of the Moon can be seen in action in Hawaii.

The Eastern Snake River Plain marks the path of the North American crustal plate as it moved over a heat source called the Yellowstone Hot Spot. It is believed that the heat source fueling Yellowstone's thermal features today is essentially the same one that produced volcanic episodes from the Oregon/Nevada/Idaho boundary to Yellowstone National Park.

of the Hawaiian Islands. According to one version of the theory, uneven heating within the Earth's core allows some material in the overlying mantle to become slightly hotter than surrounding material. As its temperature increases, its density decreases. Thus it becomes relatively buoyant and rises through the cooler materials—like a tennis ball released underwater—toward the Earth's crust. When this molten material reaches the crust, it eventually melts and pushes itself through the crust and it erupts onto the Earth's surface as molten lava.

The Earth's crust is made up of numerous plates that float upon an underlying mantle layer. Therefore, over time, the presence of an unusual heat source created by a mantle plume will be expressed at the Earth's surface—floating in a constant direction above it—as a line of volcanic eruptions. The Snake River Plain records the progress of the North American crustal plate—350 miles in 15 million years—over a heat source now located below Yellowstone.

Two Stages of Volcanism. As the upwelling magma from the mantle collects in the Earth's lower crust, its heat begins to melt the surrounding crustal rock. Since this rock contains a large amount of silica, it forms a thick and pasty rhyolite magma. Rhyolite is lighter than the overlying crustal rocks, therefore, it begins to rise and form a second magma chamber very close to the Earth's surface. As more and more of this gas-charged rhyolite collects in this upper crustal chamber, the gas pressure builds to a point at which the magma explodes through the Earth's crust.

Explosive Rhyolitic Volcanism. When the gas-charged molten material reached the surface, the gas expanded rapidly, perhaps as much as 25 to 75 times by volume. The reaction is similar to the bubbles that form in a bottle of soda pop that has been shaken. You can shake the container and the bottled liquid will retain its volume as long as the cap is tightly sealed. Release the pressure by removing the bottle cap, however, and the soft drink will spray all over the room and occupy a volume of space far larger than the bottle from which it issued. This initial vast spray is then followed by a foaming action as the less gas-charged liquid now bubbles out of the bottle.

Collectively, the numerous rhyolitic explosions that occurred on the Snake River Plain ejected thousands of cubic miles of material into the atmosphere and onto the Earth's surface. In contrast, the eruption of Mount Saint Helens in 1980, which killed 65 people and devastated 150 square miles of forest, produced less than one-fourth cubic mile of ejected material. So much material was ejected in the massive rhyolitic explosions in the Snake River Plain that the Earth's surface collapsed to form huge depressions known as calderas which swallowed entire mountain ranges in the process. Most evidence of these unimaginably huge and explosive eruptions has been covered by subsequent flows of basaltic lava. However, traces of rhyolitic eruptions are visible along the margins of the plain and in the Yellowstone area.

Quiet Outpourings of Basaltic Lava. As this area of the Earth's crust passed over and then beyond the sub-surface heat source, the explosive volcanism of the rhyolitic stage ceased. The heat contained in the Earth's upper mantle and crust, however, remained and continued to produce upwelling magma. This was basaltic magma that, because it contained less silica than rhyolite, was very fluid.

The basalt, like the rhyolite, collected in isolated magma chambers within the crust until pressures built up to force it to the surface through fissures or rifts. These linear cracks formed as the result of the same crustal stretching that created the basin and range topography that surrounds the Snake River Plain.

Upon reaching the surface, the gases contained within the lava easily escaped and produced relatively mild eruptions. Instead of exploding into the air like earlier rhyolitic activity, the more fluid basaltic

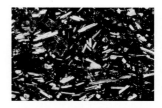
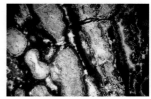

Microscopic cross sections of basaltic rock (top) and rhyolitic rock show vastly different textures. Rhyolitic magma contains more silica; it is very thick and does not allow trapped gas to escape easily. Its volcanic eruptions blast large craters in the Earth's crust. Basaltic magma is more fluid and allows gas to escape readily. It erupts more gently. Here in the eastern Snake River Plain, basaltic lava flows almost completely cover earlier rhyolitic deposits.

25

Identifying the Lava Flows

At Craters of the Moon the black rocks are lava flows. The surface lava rocks, basaltic in composition, formed from magma originating deep in the Earth. They are named for their appearances: **Pahoehoe** (pronounced "pah-hoy-hoy" and meaning "ropey"), **Aa** (pronounced "ah-ah" and meaning "rough"), or **Blocky.** Geologists have seen how these flows behave in modern volcanic episodes in Hawaii and elsewhere.

Pahoehoe. More than half the monument is covered by pahoehoe lava flows. Rivers of molten rock, they harden quickly to a relatively smooth surface, billowy, hummocky, or flat. Other pahoehoe formations resemble coiled, heavy rope or ice jams.

Aa. Aa lava flows are far more rugged than pahoehoe flows. Most occur when a pahoehoe flow cools, thickens, and then turns into aa. Often impassable to those traveling by foot, aa flows quickly chew up hiking boots. Blocky lava is a variety of aa lava whose relatively high silica content makes it thick and often dense, glassy, and smooth.

Bombs. Globs of lava ejected high in the air may solidify in flight. They are classed by shape: spindle, ribbon, cow pie, and breadcrust. Bombs range from ½-inch to more than 10 feet long.

Tree Molds. When molten lava advances on a living forest, resulting tree molds may record impressions of charred surfaces of trees in the lava.

Spindle Bomb

Tree Mold

Pahoehoe Toe

Aa Lava

Lava River

Breadcrust Bomb

Blocky Lava

Pahoehoe Ropes

Blue Dragon Lava

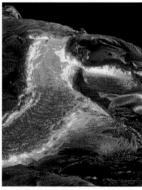

Mt. St. Helens erupts in 1980 (**top photo**). Because the lava contained a large amount of silica, its explosive eruption contrasts sharply with recent basaltic flows that formed in Hawaii (**bottom**).

lava flooded out onto the surrounding landscape. These flows covered many square miles and most of the older rhyolitic deposits.

The Great Rift and Craters of the Moon. The Great Rift is the youngest of the volcanic fissures on the Snake River Plain and the source of the greatest diversity of volcanic features found here. The Great Rift is approximately 52 miles long, stretching from the Pioneer Mountains to an area just north of the Snake River. It is composed of a series of parallel cracks, some of which have been measured to a depth of more than 600 feet.

Eight Major Eruptive Periods. The Craters of the Moon lava field formed between 2,000 and 15,000 years ago in a series of basaltic eruptions. Eight eruptive periods, each lasting about 1,000 years, were separated by periods of relative calm that lasted for a few hundred to more than 2,000 years. These sequences of eruptions and calm periods are caused by the alternating build up and release of magmatic pressure inside the Earth. Once an eruption releases this pressure, time is required for it to build up again.

Eruptions have been dated by two methods: paleomagnetic and radiometric dating. Paleomagnetic dating compares the alignment of magnetic minerals within the rock of flows with past orientations of the Earth's magnetic fields to provide relative dates for different lava formations. Radiometric dating methods have been used to determine ages of younger flows at Craters of the Moon by measuring the relative percentages of Carbon-14 isotopes from charcoal samples preserved within lava flows. Other radioactive isotopes have been measured to estimate the age of older flows like the 425,000 year old Laidlaw Butte shield volcano.

A Typical Eruption at Craters of the Moon. Research at the monument and observations of similar eruptions in Hawaii and Iceland suggest the following scenario for a typical eruption at Craters of the Moon. When the forces that tend to pull the Earth's crust apart are combined with the forces created as magma accumulates, the crust becomes weakened and cracks form. As the magma rises buoyantly within these cracks, the pressure exerted on it is reduced and the gases within the magma begin to expand. As gas continues to expand, the magma becomes frothy.

At first the lava is very fluid and charged with gas. Eruptions begin as a long line of fountains that can be over a mile in length. This "curtain of fire eruption" mainly produces cinders and frothy, fluid lava. After hours or days, the amount of gas decreases and eruptions become less violent. As segments of the fissure seal off and eruptions become more localized, fountains of gas charged lava may squirt as high as 2,000 feet into the air. As these cinders rain down into piles around or near individual vents they form cinder cones.

With further reductions in the gas content of the magma, the volcanic activity again changes. Huge outpourings of lava are pumped out of the various fissures or the vents of cinder cones and form lava flows. Lava flows may form over periods of months or possibly a few years. Long-term eruptions of lava flows from a single vent become the source of most of the material produced during a sustained eruption. As gas pressure falls and magma is depleted, flows subside. Finally, all activity stops.

When Will the Next Eruption Occur? Craters of the Moon is not an extinct volcanic area. It is merely in a dormant stage of its eruptive sequence. By dating the lava flows, geologists have shown that the volcanic activity along the Great Rift has been persistent over the last 15,000 years, occurring approximately every 2,000 years. Because the last eruptions took place about 2,000 years ago, geologists believe that eruptions are due here again—probably within the next 1,000 years.

From the air, the Great Rift looks like an irregularly dashed line punctuated by tell-tale cones and craters (**top**). It is actually a band of parallel cracks that extend southward from the Pioneer Mountains for 52 miles. Fissure eruptions along crack systems are common in Hawaii (**bottom**).

Indian Tunnel

Indian Tunnel is a cave technically called a lava tube. When a pahoehoe lava flow is exposed to the air, its surface begins to cool and harden. A crust or skin develops. As the flow moves away from its source, the crust thickens and forms an insulating barrier between cool air and molten material in the flow's interior. Like an iced-over river in winter, a rigid roof now exists over the stream of lava whose molten core continues to move forward. As the flow of lava in the tube wanes, the level of lava within the molten core gradually begins to drop. The flowing interior then pulls away from the hardening roof above and slowly drains away and out. The roof and last remnants of the lava river inside it cool and harden, leaving a tube.

Many lava tubes make up the Indian Tunnel Lava Tube System. These tubes formed during the same eruption within a single lava flow whose source was a fissure or crack in the Spatter Cones area. A tremendous amount of lava was pumped out here, forming the Blue Dragon Flows. These flows were named for the blue coloration that is produced when light strikes the glassy glaze on the surface of the lava.

Ice Stalactites

Lava forced through the roof of the tube system formed huge ponds whose surfaces cooled and began to harden. Later these ponds collapsed as the lava drained back into the lava tubes. Big Sink is the largest of these collapses. The Blue Dragon Flow covers an area of more than 100 square miles. Hidden beneath are miles of lava tubes, but collapsed roof sections called skylights provide entry to only a small part of the system. Only time, with the collapse of more rocks, will reveal the total extent of the system.

Stalactites. Dripped from hot ceilings, lava forms stalactites that hang from above. **Mineral deposits.** Sulfate compounds formed on many lava tube ceilings from volcanic gases or by evaporation of water as it is leached from rocks above. **Ice.** In spring, ice stalactites form on the cave ceilings and walls. Ice stalagmites form on the cave floor. Summer heat destroys these features in most caves. **Wildlife.** Lava tube beetles, bushy-tailed woodrats (packrats), and bats live in some dark caves. Violet-green swallows, great horned owls, and ravens may use wall cracks and shelves of well-lit caves for nesting sites.

Lava Stalactites

Cinder Cones and Spatter Cones

Cinder Cones. When volcanic eruptions of fairly moderate strength throw cinders into the air, cinder cones may be built up. These cone-shaped hills are usually truncated, looking as though their tops were sliced off. Usually, a bowl- or funnel-shaped crater will form inside the cone. Cinders which cooled rapidly while falling through the air, are highly porous with gas vesicles, like bubbles. Cinder cones hundreds of feet high may be built in a few days. Big Cinder Butte is a cinder cone. At 700 feet high, it is the tallest cone in the monument. The shape develops because the largest fragments, and in fact most of the fragments, fall closest to the vent. The angle of slope is usually about 30 degrees. Some cinder cones, such as North Crater, the Watchman, and Sheep Trail Butte, were built by more than one volcanic episode. Younger lava was added to them as a vent was rejuvenated. If strong winds prevail during a cinder cone's formation, the cone may be elongated—in the direction the wind was blowing—rather than being circular. Grassy, Paisley, Sunset, and Inferno Cones are elongated to the east because the dominant winds in this area come from the west.

The northernmost section of the Great Rift contains the most cinder cones for three reasons: 1. There were more eruptions at that end of the rift. 2. The lavas erupted there were thicker (because they contain more silica), resulting in more explosive eruptions. 3. Large amounts of ground water may have been present at the northern boundary of the lavas and, where it came in contact with magma, it generated huge amounts of steam. All of these conditions lead to more extensive and explosive eruptions that tend to create cinder cones rather than lava flows.

Spatter Cones. When most of its gas content has dissipated, lava becomes less frothy and more tacky. Then it is tossed out of the vent as globs or clots of lava paste called spatter. The clots partially weld together to build up spatter cones. Spatter cones are typically much smaller than cinder cones, but they may have steeper sides. The Spatter Cones area of the monument contains one of the most perfect spatter-cone chains in the world. These cones are generally less than 100 feet high and a few hundred feet in diameter.

Life Adapts to a Volcanic Landscape

Two thousand years after volcanic eruptions subsided, plants and animals still struggle to gain toeholds on these unforgiving lava fields. Much of the world's vegetation could not survive here at all. Environmental stresses created by scant soil and minimal moisture are compounded by highly porous cinders that are incapable of holding water near the ground surface where plants and other organisms can make ready use of it. Scarce at best—total average precipitation is between 12 to 16 inches per year—rainwater and snowmelt quickly slips down out of reach of the plants growing on cinder cones. Summer's hot, dry winds rob moisture from all living things exposed to them. On the side of a cinder cone, summer day temperatures at ground level can be more than 150°F.

The secret to survival here is adaptation. Most life forms cope by strategies of either resisting or evading the extremes of this semi-arid climate. To resist being robbed of moisture by winds and heat, a plant may feature very small leaves that minimize moisture loss. To evade heat, wind, and aridity, another plant may grow inside a crevice that provides life-giving shade and collects precious moisture and soil particles. Another plant may spend about 95-percent of the year dormant. It may rush through the germination, sprouting, leafing out, blooming, and fruiting stages and return to the dormancy of its seed stage in just two weeks. The dwarf buckwheat has adapted to life on porous cinders by evolving a root system that spreads out for up to three feet to support its above ground part, which is a mere four inches high. This buckwheat only looks like a dwarf because you cannot see its roots.

Environmental conditions at Craters of the Moon are generally so harsh that slight changes can make the difference between survival or death of a plant or other organism. Life thrives in many rock crevices that are

Lichens often pioneer new life on Earth. Two plants in one, lichens are composed of an alga and a fungus growing together for their mutual benefit, usually on rock. Hardy and slow-growing, lichens help break down rock to soil-building mineral matter.

Eventually their vegetable matter decays, helping to form the first soils that plants can use. Tough in the extreme, some lichens can be heated to high temperatures and still be capable of resuming normal growth when returned to viable conditions.

Plants Adapt to a Volcanic Landscape

Water is a limiting factor in plant growth and reproduction both on the lava fields of Craters of the Moon and on the surrounding sagebrush steppe. Plants have developed a combination of adaptations to cope with drought conditions. There are three major strategies:

1. Drought tolerance.
Physiological adaptations leading to drought tolerance are typical of desert plant species. The tissues of some plants can withstand extreme dehydration without suffering permanent cell damage. Some plants can extract water from very dry soils. Sagebrush and antelope bitterbrush exemplify drought tolerance.

2. Drought avoidance.
Certain structural modifications can enable plants to retain or conserve water. Common adaptations of this type include small leaves, hairiness, and succulence. The small leaves of the antelope bitterbrush expose less area to evaporation influences such as heat and wind.

Light-colored hairs on the scorpionweed reduce surface evaporation by inhibiting air flow and reflecting sunlight. Succulent plants such as the

Prickly Pear Cactus

Scorpionweed

prickly pear cactus have tissues that can store water for use during drought periods. Other plants, such as wire lettuce, avoid drought by having very little leaf surface compared to their overall volume.

3. Drought escape. Some plants, such as mosses and ferns, escape drought by grow-ing near persistent water sup-plies associated with cracks and overhangs. Many other drought escapers, such as dwarf monkeyflower, simply carry out their full life cycle during the moist time of the year. The rest of the year they survive in seed form.

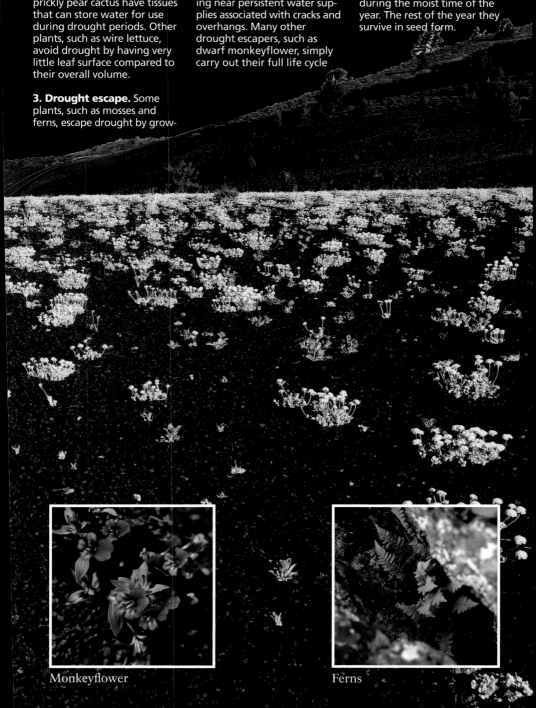

Monkeyflower

Ferns

Plant Habitats

Lava Flows. Most plants cannot grow on lava flows until enough soil has accumulated to support them. Soils first form from the eroded lava and the slow decomposition of lichens and other plants able to colonize the bare rock. These soils are supplemented by wind-blown soil particles until vascular plants gain footholds. As plants begin to grow and then die, their gradual decomposition adds further soil matter. These soil beginnings accumulate in cracks and crevices, which also provide critical moisture, shade, and wind protection. Deep crevices provide lower temperatures favoring plant survival. Shallow crevices will hold scabland penstemon, fernleaf fleabane, and gland cinquefoil. Deep crevices can support syringa, various ferns, bush rockspirea, fern bush, and even limber pine. Not until full soil cover is achieved can the antelope bitterbrush, rubber rabbitbrush, and sagebrush find suitable niches.

Cinder Gardens. Compared to lava flows, cinder cones are much more quickly invaded by plants. Here too, however, volcanic origins influence plant growth. Compared to the relatively level lava flows, steeply sloping cinder cones introduce a new factor that controls the development of plant communities: topography. Here you find marked differences in the plant communities between the north- and south-facing slopes. South-facing slopes are

Lava Flow

exposed to prolonged, intense sunlight, resulting in high evaporation of water. Because of prevailing winds, snow accumulates on northeast sides of the cones, giving them far more water than southwest-facing sides receive. The pioneering herbs that first colonize cinder cones will persist on southwest-facing slopes long after succeeding plant communities have come to dominate north-facing slopes. It is on these north-facing slopes that limber pine, and occasionally aspen groves, may develop.

Kipukas. Ironically, the same searing lava flows that destroyed everything in their path now protect some of the last remaining islands of healthy, intact sagebrush-steppe vegetation on the Snake River Plain. These features are called kipukas, a variation of the Hawaiia term "puka" that means The 500 plus kipukas with the monument vary in siz and integrity. The best on are living examples of nat plant communities largely unaffected by livestock g ing and non-native plants They provide important baseline data for monum staff in their efforts to pr and restore native vegeta

ipuka

Limber pines are the tree pioneers of the lava terrain. Young seedlings **(top)** often find suitable conditions for germinating in rock crevices long before the surrounding landscapes can support tree growth. Most common of all the monument's trees, limber pine is named for its flexible branches. Many animals depend on this tree in some fashion for their livelihoods. Limber pine cones turn brown and woody as their seeds mature in the second year of growth. Cones grow to about four inches in length **(bottom)**.

surrounded by barren, exposed lava rock of the same physical composition. These microhabitats provide the critical shade, soil, and moisture required for plant survival. Over the years, particles of soil will naturally collect in rock crevices, which also have the effect of funneling precipitation into their depths. Their shade further protects these pockets of soil and water from wind erosion, excessive heat, evaporation, and leaching by direct sunlight.

At Craters of the Moon, crevices are of such importance to plants that botanists differentiate between narrow, shallow, and deep crevices when studying this phenomenon. Narrow crevices will support dwarf goldenweed or hairy goldenaster. Shallow crevices support scabland penstemon, fernleaf fleabane, and gland cinquefoil. Deep crevices give rise to syringa, ferns, rockspirea, fern bush, and even the limber pine tree. Complete soil cover and then vegetative cover can develop on these lava flows only after crevices have first become filled with soil.

Plants exploit other means of protection to survive in this harsh environment. Shaded and wind-sheltered, the northern side of a cinder cone can support grass, shrubs, and limber pine trees while the cone's southern face supports only scattered herbs. Most cinder cones in the park show distinct differences of plant cover between their northern and southern exposures. Northern exposures are cooler and moister than southern exposures, which receive far more direct sunlight. In addition, here at Craters of the Moon, the prevailing southwesterly winds compound the ability of the dry heat to rob porous cinder cone surfaces and their living organisms of precious moisture.

The build-up of successive lava flows has so raised the landscape that it now intercepts wind currents that operate higher above surrounding plains. Limber pine trees find footholds on the shaded and sheltered northern exposures of cinder cones. Bitterbrush and rabbitbrush shrubs are much more abundant on the protected northern face of the cones. For many species of plants, the limits of habitability on this volcanic landscape are narrowly defined. Very small variations in their situations can determine success or failure.

Travelers often ask park rangers whether or not some of the park's plants were planted by people. The plants in question are dwarf buckwheats growing in cinder gardens. It is their incredibly even spacing that creates an orderliness that is easy to mistake for human design. The regular spacing is the result of the competition for moisture, however. The root systems of these plants exploit the available water from an area of ground surface much larger than the spread of their foliage. In this way, mature plants can fend off competition by using the moisture that would be required for a potentially encroaching plant to become established. The effect is an even spacing that makes it appear, indeed, as though someone had set out the plants on measured centers.

Craters of the Moon abounds with these surprising plant microhabitats that delight explorers on foot. The bleak lava flows separate these emerging pockets of new life, isolating them like islands or oases within their barren volcanic surroundings.

Scientists have studied Carey Kipuka to find out what changes have occurred in this isolated biological community. Kipuka is an Hawaiian name given to an area of older land that is surrounded by younger lava flows. Recent lava flows did not overrun Carey Kipuka, so its plant cover is unaltered. Shortage of water protected it from livestock grazing that might have changed its character. Its vegetation is a benchmark for comparing plant cover changes on similar sites throughout southern Idaho.

For the National Park Service and other managers of wildlands, kipukas—representing isolated and pristine plant habitat unchanged by human influence—provide the best answer that we have to the important question, "What is natural?" Armed with a satisfactory answer to that question, it is possible to manage the land ecologically. Monument managers can seek to restore natural systems and to allow them to be as self-regulating as possible. It is ironic that Craters of the Moon, a volcanic landscape subjected to profound change, should also protect this informative glimpse of what remains unchanged.

The American pika (Ochontona princeps) is a small mammal closely related to the rabbit. They are generally found in talus and rock piles in mountainous habitats, but find the crack-ridden lava flows can also be a good place to live. The lava crevices provide shelter from predators, the hot summer sun, and harsh winter storms.

Pikas harvest grasses, forbs, and shrubs during the summer and then dry them on the hot surface of the lava. These piles of drying, curing vegetation are called "hay-stacks." This plant material is later stored beneath the ground to be eaten in the winter.

Scientists are monitoring pikas within the monument to determine if climate change is having an impact on their distribution and

Wildflowers

Wildflowers carpet Craters of the Moon's seemingly barren lava fields from early May to late September. The most spectacular floral blooms come with periods of precipitation. In late spring, moisture from snowmelt—supplemented now and then by rainfall—sees the blossoming of most of the delicate annual plants.

Many of the monument's flowering plants, having no mechanisms for conserving moisture, simply complete their life cycles before the middle of summer. This is particularly true of those that grow on the porous cinder gardens into which moisture quickly descends beyond reach of most plants' root systems.

As summer continues and supplies of moisture slowly dwindle, only the most drought-resistant of flowering plants continue to grow and to bloom. With the onset of autumn, only the tiny yellow blossoms of the rabbitbrush remain.

Evening primrose

Phlox

Sego lily

Indian paintbrush

Blue penstemon

Blazing star

Bitterroot

Wild onion

of the largest ecosystems
ne West is so vast it is
netimes described as a
gebrush sea." This ecosys-
n is so named because
ebrush is the dominant
nt growing on this high
ert plain (or steppe). Over
years, a variety of different
uences have had an ad-
se impact on this land-
pe. Overgrazing, wildfires,
introduction of exotic
nts, and, most of all, wide-
ead development by hu-

mans, have all resulted in a
significant loss of healthy
sagebrush habitat.

This loss of habitat has caused
concern about the future of
some species of wildlife that
live in these areas. Many animals are affected by the loss of
sagebrush, but two species are
especially susceptible because
of their nearly complete depen-
dence on the plant. These are
the Greater sage-grouse (Cen-
trocercus urophasianus) and

the pygmy rabbit (Brachylagus
idahoensis).

Sage-grouse. No animal
depends so completely on the
sagebrush environment as the
sage-grouse. This bird relies on
sagebrush to provide cover for
breeding, nesting, and protection from predators. It is also a
major source of food in the
summer and 99-percent of its
diet in the winter. Over the past
50 years, biologists have seen a
dramatic decrease in the num-

Sage-grouse

Idaho and the West. They are now considered a "sensitive" species.

Pygmy Rabbit. The smallest rabbit in North America, the pygmy rabbit, is also completely dependant on the availability of sagebrush. It is the rabbit's primary food source, provides shelter, and can be found in the winter when nothing else is available. A drop in the number of these animals is suspected but

not yet confirmed by research. What is known is that the rabbit is no longer found in many areas where it had traditionally lived. This may be because the loss of sagebrush-steppe habitat has caused a fragmentation of the rabbit's habitat that prevents them from expanding into new areas or maintaining isolated populations.

The importance of protecting sagebrush-steppe is now critical if many wildlife species are

to survive. As their names imply, the sage thrasher, sage sparrow, sagebrush lizard, and the sagebrush vole all rely on a healthy sagebrush community. At Craters of the Moon, the sage-brush steppe covers 340,000 acres within the monument—roughly one-half of the entire monument. As the sagebrush-steppe landscape throughout the West continues to deteriorate, it becomes more and more important that it be protected here.

Pygmy rabbit

American Indians, Explorers, and Astronauts

Few people have chosen to stay long on the hot, dry, and seemingly unending lava terrain that makes up Craters of the Moon. Native Americans traveled through the monument for thousands of years, but only in connection with annual migrations to more hospitable places. Emigrants travelling west on Goodale's Cutoff could not wait to get through this place where water was hard to find and travel by wagon was difficult. Geologists ventured into the area, but their stays were marked by difficult challenges and were always short lived. Astronauts visited the monument only because they felt experiencing its harshly alien environment would give them a better understanding of geologic features on the moon. No one remained for long on the desolate lava flows.

American Indians traversed this area each spring on their way to the food-rich Camas Prairie and, eventually, to net salmon on the Snake River. Their routes were marked by well-worn foot-trails and many sites where artifacts of Shoshone and Bannock cultures have been found. Most of these archeological sites are not easily discerned by the untrained eye, but the stone rings at Indian Tunnel are easily examined. These circles of rocks may have been used for temporary shelter, hunting blinds, or religious purposes. Numerous stone tools, and the hammerstones and flakes from arrowhead making are found scattered throughout the lava flows. Some of the harder, denser volcanic materials found here were made into cutting and scraping tools and projectile points. Such evidence suggests only short forays into the lavas for hunting or plant collecting by small groups.

The Shoshone and Bannock people were a hunting and gathering culture directly dependent on what the land offered. They turned what they could of this volcanic environment to their benefit. Before settlement by Europeans, the vicinity of the monument boasted several animal species that are rare or absent

The Shoshone-Bannock regularly passed through the Craters of the Moon area on their annual summer migration from the Snake River to the Camas Prairie, west of the monument. They took this journey to get out of the hot desert and into the cooler mountains. There they could gather plants and roots and hunt rabbits, marmots, porcupines and ground squirrels. As they passed through today's monument, they left behind arrowheads, choppers, and scrapers. They also built stone circles (see photo) that may have been used for ceremonial purposes. These artifacts and structures are evidence that people utilized this vast volcanic landscape.

from Craters of the Moon today. These included wolf, bison, grizzly bear, and bighorn sheep, whose males sport characteristic headgear of large, curled horns, have been absent from the monument since about 1920.

Military explorer U.S. Army Capt. B.L.E. Bonneville left impressions of the Craters of the Moon lava field in his travel diaries in the early 1800s. In The Adventures of Captain Bonneville, which were based on the diaries, 19th-century author Washington Irving provided an early, if brief, glimpse of a then unnamed Craters of the Moon, in writing that this was a place "where nothing meets the eye but a desolate and awful waste, where no grass grows nor water runs, and where nothing is to be seen but lava." Irving is perhaps most famous for The Legend of Sleepy Hollow, but his Adventures is considered a significant period work about the West.

Early pioneers who left traces in the vicinity of the park did so by following what eventually came to be known as Goodale's Cutoff. The route was based on Indian trails that skirted the lava fields in the northern section of the park. It came into use in the early 1850s as an alternate to the regular route of the Oregon Trail. Shoshone-Bannock hostilities along the Snake River portion of the trail—one such incident is memorialized in Idaho's Massacre Rocks State Park—led the emigrants to search for a safer route. They were headed for Oregon, particularly the Walla Walla area around Whitman Mission. They traveled in family groups in search of agricultural lands for settlement. Emigrants traveling the route in 1854 noticed names carved in rocks and trees. It was named in 1862 by travelers apparently grateful to their guide, Tim Goodale, whose presence, they felt, had prevented Indian attacks. Massachusetts-born Goodale was cut in the mold of the typical early trapper and trader of the Far West. He was known to the famous fur trade brothers Solomon and William Sublette. His name turned up at such fur trade locales as Pueblo, Taos, Fort Bridger, and Fort Laramie over a period of at least 20 years.

After the discovery of gold in Idaho's Salmon River country, a party of emigrants persuaded Goodale to guide them over the route they would name for him. Goodale was an experienced guide: in 1861, he had served in that capacity for a military survey west of Denver. The large band of emigrants set out in July and was joined by more wagons at Craters of the Moon. Eventually their numbers included 795 men and 300 women and children. Indian attacks occurred frequently along the Oregon Trail at that time, but the size of this group evidently discouraged such incursions. The trip was not without incident, but Goodale's reputation remained sufficiently intact for his clients to affix his name to the route. Subsequent modifications and the addition of a ferry crossing on the Snake River made Goodale's Cutoff into a popular route for western emigration. Traces of it are still visible in the vicinity of the monument today.

Curiosity about this uninhabitable area eventually led to more detailed knowledge of Craters of the Moon and knowledge led to its preservation. Geologists Israel C. Russell and Harold T. Stearns of the U.S. Geological Survey explored here in 1901 and 1923, respectively. Taxidermist-turned-lecturer, Robert Limbert, explored the area in the early 1920s. Limbert made several trips into the monument. On early visits, he more or less retraced the steps of these geologists. Later, on his most ambitious trek, Limbert and W. L. Cole traversed the Great Rift south to north, starting from the nearby community of Minidoka. These explorations and their attendant publicity in National Geographic Magazine were instrumental in the proclamation of Craters of the Moon as a national monument by President Calvin Coolidge in 1924.

Since Limbert's day, astronauts have walked both here and on the moon. Despite our now detailed knowledge of the differences between these two places, the name–and much of the monument's awe-inspiring appeal–remains the same. It is as though by learning more about both these niches in our universe we somehow have learned more about ourselves as well.

In the mid-1800s, the Oregon Trail served as a major route to the West for emigrants. But when hostilities developed along the trail with the Shoshone-Bannocks, many of the pioneers began using an alternate route known as Goodale's Cutoff. This trail went further north and passed through the present-day monument.

The first recorded exploration of these lava fields was conducted by two Arco, Idaho cattlemen in 1879. Arthur Ferris and J.W. Powell were looking for water for their livestock. The first scientific explorations were carried out by Israel C. Russell, surveying the area for the U.S. Geologic Survey (USGS) in 1901 and 1903. Beginning in 1910, Samuel A. Paisley, later to become the monument's first custodian, also explored these lava fields. In 1921, the USGS sent two geologists, Harold T. Stearns and O.E. Meinzer, to this area. Stearns recommended that a national monument be created here. Also during the early 20s, the exploration of Idaho adventurer Robert W. Limbert caught the public's fancy. A report of the explorations of "Two-gun" Bob Limbert was published in the March 1924 National Geographic Magazine. Limbert was a Boise, Idaho taxidermist, tanner, and furrier. He was also a quick draw artist who later performed on the national lecture circuit. Reportedly, Limbert once challenged Al Capone to a pistol duel at 10 paces. Evidently, Capone declined. Limbert made several treks into the lava fields between 1921 and 1926. He first explored the more easily accessible northern portion of the lava fields. In 1920, Limbert traversed the entire Great Rift from south to north, starting from Minidoka, Idaho.

and an Airedale terrier. Taking the dog along was a mistake. Limbert wrote, "For after three days travel his feet were worn raw and bleeding." Limbert said it was pitiful to watch the dog as it hobbled after them. The landscape was so unusual that Limbert and Cole had difficulty estimating distances. Things would be half again as far away as they had reckoned. In some areas their compass needles went wild with magnetic distortions caused by high concentrations of iron in the lava rocks.

Bizarre features they found— such as multi-colored, blow-out craters—moved Limbert to write, "I noticed that at places like these we had almost nothing to say." Limbert and Cole discovered ice caves with ice stalactites. They found water by tracking the flights of mourning doves.

They found pockets of cold water (trapped above ground by ice deposits below the surface) covered by yellowjackets fatally numbed by the cold. They drank the water anyway. "In desert country," said Limbert, "one can't be too picky." Between Limbert's lively article—Among the Craters of the Moon—and the reports of geologist Stearns, President Calvin Coolidge was induced to designate part of the lava fields as Craters of the Moon National Monument on May 2, 1924

The Limbert Trek
On his third expedition, Limbert, Cole, and a dog traversed the lava flows from south to north. The photos that appeared in National Geographic Magazine in 1924 were taken on various

Robert W. Limbert

Approaching Craters of the Moon

Craters of the Moon National Monument and Preserve is located in south-central Idaho's Snake River Plain, midway between Boise, Idaho and Grand Teton and Yellowstone National Parks. The monument includes over 750,000 acres, and the elevation at the visitor center is 5,900 feet above sea level. U.S. 20-26-93 provides access to the visitor center, campground, and scenic loop road. Nominal entrance fees are charged. Interagency passes are honored and may be obtained at the entrance station.

Seasons and Weather. The visitor center is open year-round, with the exception of winter holidays. From November to April, the loop road is closed to vehicle traffic and becomes a winter trail for skiing and snowshoeing. In spring and fall, the opening and closing of the loop road are determined by weather conditions, which vary greatly from year to year. In the spring, the weather is unpredictable. Strong winds may occur and snow and/or freezing rain are not uncommon. Temperatures range from highs in the 50s to lows in the 20s°F. Summer means warm to hot days and cool nights. Expect afternoon winds. There may be very sporadic afternoon thunderstorms, and temperatures may range from the 40s to 90s°F. Fall generally offers fair weather with low precipitation and infrequent winds. Early snowstorms are possible, and snow is certain by late fall. Fall temperatures range from highs in the 60s to lows in the 30s°F. Winter brings the possibility of severe storms with drifting snow. Highway access is often best described as snowpacked. On bright, sunny days temperatures may reach into the 40s°F, but the range is generally from highs in the 30s to lows around minus 10°F.

Accessibility. The visitor center, restrooms, and amphitheater are wheelchair accessible. Audio-visual presentations at the visitor center are also accessible for the hearing impaired. The trails at the Spatter Cones and Devil's Orchard are accessible. There is also a wheelchair accessible campsite in the campground. Signs at each trailhead provide additional information about accessibility.

Travel Planning. U.S. 20-26-93 provides access to the Craters of the Moon visitor center and Loop Road. No public transportation services the Monument. Scheduled airlines serve Boise, Idaho Falls, Pocatello, Twin Falls, and Hailey, Idaho. Rental cars are generally available at these airports, but advanced reservations are advised. It is about a four-hour drive from the Monument to Grand Teton or Yellowstone National Park. Idaho's travel office provides information about cultural activities, scenic tours, outfitters and guides, chambers of commerce, hotels, and motels throughout the state. Visit their website at www. visitidaho.org or telephone 1-800-VIS-ITID.

Roads. Off-road travel is prohibited throughout the Monument. Please stay on roadways and parking pulloffs that are provided. When traveling on backcountry roads, the use of a high-clearance, four-wheel drive vehicle is recommended. Without a map (available at both BLM and NPS offices), the road system in the backcountry may be confusing in the BLM Monument. Win-

Make the visitor center **(top)** your first stop in the monu-ment. Ask at the information desk for schedules of ranger-led walks, talks, and other programs and for

ter travel on these roads can be difficult or impossible. Carry a fire extinguisher and shovel and be prepared to use them in an emergency during dry summer months.

Information about the Monument.

Superintendent
Craters of the Moon National
Monument and Preserve
P.O. Box 29
Arco, ID 83213
or
Monument Manager
Craters of the Moon National
Monument
Bureau of Land Management
Shoshone Field Office
400 W. F Street
Shoshone, ID 83352.

Telephone.
NPS: 208-527-1335
BLM: 208-732-7200

Email.
NPS: crmo_information@nps.gov
BLM: id_so_information@blm.gov

Websites.
NPS:
www.nps.gov/crmo

BLM:
www.blm.gov/id/st/en/fo/shoshone/
special_areas/Craters.html

Visitor Center and Programs

The visitor center near the scenic seven-mile Loop Road is located at the main entrance to the monument. Here you will find displays and information to help you plan your visit. The Craters of the Moon Natural History Association sells books, postcards, maps, and other publications at the book store. Rangers at the information counter can answer your questions and help you plan your stay in the monument.

The displays alert you to wildflowers and wildlife you might expect to see here. Other exhibits describe the monument's geologic history. A video explains how lava erupted from fissures in the Earth to create the cinder cones, lava flows, and other volcanic features that you will see at Craters of the Moon. Other films are shown on a regular basis in the visitor center auditorium. Check at the visitor center for schedules of guided walks and campground programs. You can also get information here about self-guiding nature trails and the monument's loop drive.

Activities and Evening Programs. Ranger-guided walks and other programs give visitors an intimate look at various aspects of the monument. Program schedules vary; we suggest that you check the website or contact the monument for current information prior to your arrival.

Self-guiding Trails. Explore four representative areas of the monument on self-guiding nature trails. **Devils Orchard Trail** helps you understand the complex environmental concerns facing Craters of the Moon. You can walk this trail in about 20 minutes. **North Cra-** ter Flow Trail takes you through a lava flow that includes rafted blocks (crater wall fragments) and other interesting features characteristic of basaltic lava flows, which are explained by wayside exhibits. This trail goes through one of the most recent lava flows in the monument. The shiny lava flows made early explorers think the volcanic eruptions had happened only a few years before. Please stay on the trails in this very fragile area. **The Broken Top Loop Trail** is a 1.8-mile-long hike that takes you through a variety of different volcanic formations as well as several different plant and animal habitats. This trail also allows you to see a lava tube, pahoehoe toes, a cinder cone, and several types of lava flows. A guide is available at the trailhead. **The Caves Trail** allows you the opportunity to explore a lava tube. These caves formed when the surface of a lava flow cooled and hardened while the interior remained molten and continued to drain. After the lava drained away, a hollow tube remained. A pamphlet at the trailhead provides a map of the cave area and tells you what to expect as you explore these lava tubes on your own. Wayside exhibits point out the most interesting lava formations along the trail. To see only Indian Tunnel, the largest of the lava tubes, requires nearly one hour.

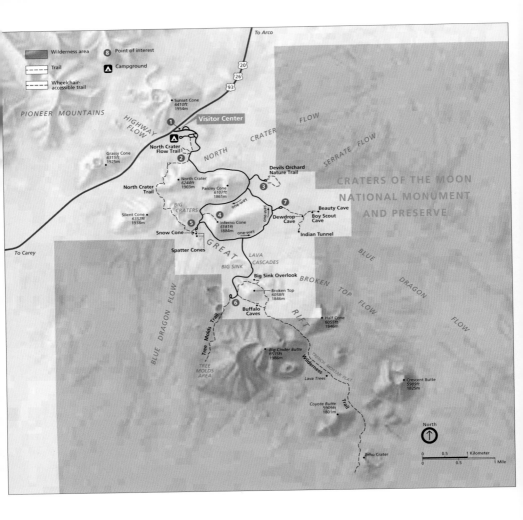

To Arco

Wilderness area   **⑧** Point of interest

⸺ ⸺ Trail   **▲** Campground

⸺ ⸺ Wheelchair-accessible trail

PIONEER MOUNTAINS

Sunset Cone
6410ft
1954m

HIGHWAY FLOW

①

Visitor Center

CRATER FLOW

NORTH

North Crater Flow Trail

②

Grassy Cone
6315ft
1925m

Devils Orchard Nature Trail

SERRATE FLOW

CRATERS OF THE MOON
NATIONAL MONUMENT
AND PRESERVE

North Crater
6244ft
1903m

North Crater Trail

Paisley Cone
6107ft
1861m

③

one-way

⑦

Beauty Cave

Boy Scout Cave

Silent Cone
6352ft
1938m

BIG CRATERS

Inferno Cone
6181ft
1884m

④

⑤

one-way

Dewdrop Cave

Snow Cone

GREAT

Spatter Cones

one-way

Indian Tunnel

LAVA CASCADES

BLUE

BIG SINK

DRAGON

Big Sink Overlook

BROKEN TOP FLOW

FLOW

Broken Top
6058ft
1846m

BLUE DRAGON FLOW

⑥

Buffalo Caves

RIFT

Half Cone
6055ft
1846m

Tree Molds Trail

TREE MOLDS AREA

Big Cinder Butte
6515ft
1986m

Wilderness

Lava Trees

Crescent Butte
5989ft
1825m

Coyote Butte
5909ft
1801m

Trail

North

Echo Crater

0   0.5   1 Kilometer
0   0.5   1 Mile

To Carey

58

Take the Driving Tour

You can see most of the features for which Craters of the Moon is famous by a combined auto and foot tour along the Loop Road. With several short walks included, you can make the drive in about two hours. Numbered stops are keyed to the map in the monument folder.

1. Visitor Center. The seven-mile Loop Road begins at the visitor center. Most of the drive is one-way. Spur roads and trailheads enable you to explore this lava field even further.

2. North Crater Flow. A short foot trail crosses the North Crater Flow to a group of crater wall fragments. This is one of the youngest flows here. The triple twist tree and its 1,350 growth rings helped early geologists estimate the age of this flow. Along this trail you can see fine examples of pahoehoe lava, pressure ridges, and squeeze-ups. Just beyond the North Crater Flow Trail is the North Crater Trail. This 1¾-mile (one way) trail ultimately leads to the Spatter Cones area.

3. Devils Orchard. Devils Orchard is a group of lava fragments that stand like islands in a sea of cinders. This marks the resting place for blocks of material from the wall of North Crater that broke free and were rafted here on lava flows. The short spur road leads to a self-guiding trail through these weird features. You can easily walk the trail in about 20 minutes. An early morning or evening visit may allow you to observe monument wildlife. In springtime, the wildflower displays in the cinder gardens are glorious. In June and early July, dwarf monkeyflowers give the ground a magenta cast.

4. Inferno Cone Viewpoint. From the overlook, a landscape of volcanic cinder cones spreads before you to the distant mountain ranges beyond. Notice that the cooler, moister northern slopes of the cones bear noticeably more vegetation than the drier southern slopes, which receive the brunt of the sunshine. If you take the short, steep walk to the summit of Inferno Cone, you can easily recognize the chain of cinder cones that defines the Great Rift. Perhaps nowhere else in the monument is it so easy to visualize how the volcanic activity broke out along this volcanic fissure in the Earth. Towering in the distance above the lava plain is Big Cinder Butte, one of the world's largest, purely basaltic, cinder cones.

5. Big Craters and Spatter Cones Area. Spatter cones formed along the Great Rift fissure where clots of pasty lava stuck together when they fell. A short trail takes you inside the best spatter cone in the chain. A steep walk to the top of Big Craters offers a view of a series of nested volcanic vents.

6. Trails to Tree Molds, Broken Top, and the Wilderness Area. A spur road just beyond the Spatter Cones takes you to a trailhead for several different trails. The Tree Molds Trail leads to an area where molten lava flows encased trees and then hardened. The cylindrical molds that remain after the wood burned and rotted away range from a few inches to more that one foot in diameter. The Broken Top Trail leads around a cinder cone and passes through a wide variety of lava formations and habitats. The Wilderness Trail takes you into the backcountry of the monument. A permit is needed to stay overnight in this area.

7. Caves Area. At this final stop on the Loop Road, a ½-mile walk takes you to the lava tubes. Here you can see Dewdrop, Boy Scout, Beauty Cave, and Indian Tunnel. Carry a flashlight and wear sturdy shoes.

Camping and Backcountry Use

The campground has about 50 sites. These are available on a first-come, first-served basis. Reservations are not accepted. A daily fee for camping is charged. Water and restrooms are provided in the campground, but there are no showers, dump station, or hookups. Wood fires are prohibited in the monument, but grills at each campsite may be used for charcoal fires. The campsites accommodate both RVs and tents. A separate group campround is available for larger groups. Contact monument staff to reserve this facility.

Wilderness Hiking. Some of the monument's most intriguing landscapes lie beyond the road's end in the 68-square-mile Craters of the Moon Wilderness Area. Few trails penetrate the wilderness, and these only for short distances. After the four-mile trail to Sentinel Butte runs out, you are on your own. For further exploration, you can simply follow the Great Rift and its chain of cinder cones. These landmarks help you find your way.

To explore farther afield, you should have a good topographical map and basic map skills. You can purchase such a map at the visitor center. A portable GPS unit is also very handy. All hikers who plan to stay overnight in the wilderness are required to obtain a backcountry permit, available free at the visitor center.

Campfires are prohibited in the wilderness. Carry a self-contained backpack stove and fuel. Mechanized vehicles, including bicycles, are prohibited in the wilderness area. Pets are also prohibited. Pack out everything that you pack in—and any trash you find that others have left behind. A good admonishment is: "Take only pictures, and try not to leave so much as a footprint."

Backcountry Travel. Visitors to the remote BLM Monument and NPS Preserve will find unimproved roads and a total lack of services (e.g. gas stations). Roads can be rough, rutted, dusty, or muddy and 4-wheel, high-clearance vehicles are recommended. Visitors to this area should come prepared with water, food, supplies, and a good map of the area because of the need to identify numerous unmarked secondary roads and junctions. You should also carry a fire extinguisher and shovel in your vehicle during the summer due to the possibility of a hot engine igniting dried plants. For this reason, motorized travel in this area during hot, dry, windy periods is not recommended. Winter use of this area, except by snowmobile, is discouraged. For information on roads, camping, fire restrictions, and to obtain maps, contact BLM or NPS.

Each hiker or driver should carry at least one gallon of water for each day out—even more may be necessary during the hot summer. There is no drinking water available in the backcountry. The best times for backcountry travel are May–June and September–October. Daytime temperatures are usually mild then, while the nights are cool, but you must be prepared for inclement and very cold weather during these transitional months.

Safety. Sturdy boots and long pants are necessary gear for the jagged lava flows. Bring clothing for both hot and cold weather; both can occur on the same day in this high-desert climate. Be sure to take plenty of drinking water. A hat, sunscreen, and sunglasses are also recommended.

Winter Recreation

In the winter, many people visit the monument to see the stark, black landscape covered in a blanket of white snow. During this period, the Loop Road is closed to driving.

The visitor center is open every day in the winter except for holidays. Winter hours are 8:00 a.m. to 4:30 p.m. To find out about current snow and trail conditions check the website or call the visitor center at 208-527-1335.

Skiing. When heavy snows accumulate, usually in late December, the Loop Road is groomed for cross-country skiing. Although skiing time varies with ability and snow conditions, most people can ski the entire loop in two to four hours. The best months for skiing are January and February in most winters. Temperatures range from 35° to well below 0°F. Blizzards may be encountered.

Hazards. Skiing off the Loop Road is allowed but requires caution. Most of the monument is covered by sharp, jagged lava, and snow cover may mask cracks and caverns underneath. Some slopes in the monument are steep enough to avalanche.

Snowshoeing. You can follow orange snow poles to explore a 1½-mile Snowshoe Loop Trail through the monument or venture off of the winter trails and climb a volcano.

Camping. Winter camping is permitted in the campground as well as designated parking areas. Neither the road to the campground nor the campsites are plowed so be prepared for a ¼-mile hike and camping in the snow.

Both backpackers and cross-country skiers find solitude in their respective seasons in the monument. Others may prefer ranger-led explorations of the monument's many unusual features.

Regulations and Safety

When traveling across the sharp and abrasive lava, stay on trails, and observe caution. Sturdy shoes and long pants are recommended. Exploring caves will require a flashlight. Undeveloped caves require additional safety measures including: 1) having three sources of light, 2) wearing helmets, kneepads and other protective gear, 3) wearing sturdy boots, and 4) notifying an emergency contact person who will know where you are going and when you are expected to return.

Day-use Permits. A day-use permit is required to visit NPS Monument lands that lie north of Highway 20-26-93. Obtain at the visitor center.

Pets. On NPS lands, pets are allowed only in the campground and on the loop road and must be kept on a leash at all times.

Vehicles. Off-road, motorized travel is prohibited throughout the monument. Bicycles are not permitted on trails in the NPS Monument and NPS Preserve except by permit on the northside.

For contemporary explorers the driving tour and its associated trails make the safest trek routes. Exercise great caution and close oversight of young children at all times, especially near lava tubes, vents, and cracks.

Hunting. No hunting is allowed in the NPS Monument. Maps of places where hunting is permitted are available from BLM or NPS offices. Idaho state hunting regulations apply.

Collecting. The collection, removal, or disturbance of any natural or cultural features within the monument, except animals which are legally taken while hunting in the BLM Monument or NPS Preserve, is strictly prohibited.

62

Nearby Attractions

Yellowstone National Park is world famous for its geysers and mudpots, canyons and waterfalls, and wildlife and wilderness. For information visit their website at www.nps.gov/yell or call them at 307-344-7381.

Grand Teton National Park features the spectacularly scenic Teton Range and lovely lakes at its base. For information visit the website at www.nps.gov/grte or call 307-739-3300.

Nez Perce National Historic Park includes 24 widely scattered sites in north-central Idaho that present the history of this ancestral homeland of the Nez Perce tribe. For information visit the website at www.nps.gov/nepe or call 208- 843-7009.

Hagerman Fossil Beds National Monument preserves Pliocene fossil sites along Idaho's Snake River. For information visit the website at www.nps.gov/hafo or call 208-933-4105.

Minidoka National Historic Site tells the story of the largest forced relocation in U.S. history. For information visit the website at www.nps.gov/miin or call 208-933-4105.

City of Rocks National Reserve is a fascinating landscape of monoliths, spires, and domes. For information visit the website at www.nps.gov/ciro or call 208-824-5519.

The Morley Nelson Snake River Birds of Prey National Conservation Area and the **Sacajawea Interpretive Cultural and Education Center,** are two of the many diverse areas managed by the Bureau of Land Management within Idaho. For more information visit the website at www.blm.gov/id/st or call 208-373-4000.

Yellowstone National Park

City of Rocks National Re-